VANISHING PRAIRIE

WALT DISNEY'S

VANISHING

PRAIRIE a True-Life Adventure

by Jane Werner
and the Staff of the
Walt Disney Studio

Based on the Film Narration by

James Algar

Winston Hibler

Ted Sears

SIMON AND SCHUSTER · NEW YORK

ALSO IN THIS SERIES

LIVING DESERT

Foreword

FOR more than two years our teams of photographers have rambled over the prairies of America's West, shooting more than 200,000 feet of motion picture film, more than 3,000 still photographs. Through the rugged winters of primitive country in Wyoming, they traveled with cater-pillar-treaded trucks, on snowshoes or skis. Under the Dakotas' broiling sun they sat for hours behind the scant shelter of brush blinds. They trailed the cougar, risked the charge of the buffalo, braved prairie fires, were drenched by prairie rainstorms and menaced by floods.

All this that we at the Studio might have the necessary footage to edit, mold, and build the 71-minute motion picture feature known as *Vanishing Prairie.*

This is a True-Life Adventure indeed—not only for the subjects of our film, the buffalo, cougars, prairie dogs, and the rest, but for everyone concerned. We have striven in *Vanishing Prairie* to do more than any of our previous nature films has done. Each of the others presented the way of life in some locale or among some group of animals; in the *Prairie* we do this job too. But, in addition—a most important addition, we feel—we are seizing at history in the making. We are snatching a dwindling opportunity to record on film—and here, in book form—a kind of native American life which within two human generations has been all but crowded out of existence.

We present this True-Life Adventure, *Vanishing Prairie,* as a parallel to a great era in American human history, the settlement of the West.

Walt Disney

Contents

Walt Disney Productions staff members
and associates who supplied color
photographs on the pages listed, include:

Lloyd Beebe, 43; Warren Garst, 13,
17 (top), 20, 21, 22, 27, 28, 39, 46,
47, 50, 60-61, 64, 66, 67, 71, 72, 73, 74,
75, 78, 79, 80, 81, 83, 84, 85, 86, 92, 94,
106 (bottom), 107 (top), 108, 109, 112,
117, 118, 119; N. Paul Kenworthy, Jr.,
77, 118 (top); Tom McHugh, 6-7, 14,
62, 65, 69, 88, 89, 91, 95, 96, 106 (top);
James R. Simon, 17 (bottom), 23, 25,
26, 29, 32, 33, 35, 36, 37, 38, 40-41,
42, 45, 48, 51, 52, 53, 54, 56, 57, 59, 98-99,
102, 103, 104, 105, 107 (bottom), 120.

The drawings throughout the book are by
Campbell Grant, with the exception of
those on pages 18 and 19, done by the staff
of Walt Disney Productions.

The Bright Past

On a map of North America, the Mississippi River and the Rocky Mountains roughly divide the continent into three parts.

In the east, the green of trees is spangled and dotted with the blue of rivers and of lakes. Westward stretch the wooded, tumbled mountain ranges of the Rockies, and the red desert. Roughly down the center spreads the broad, tawny strip of grass and brush that is the prairie.

The prairie of old was an almost endless sea of grass, under a vast blue bowl of sky. Toward the east the stems grew tall as a man, thick-rooted and limber to bend with the wind. Birds of a hundred varieties nested among the grasses, marshy with spring rains, and pecked at their nourishing seeds in the hot, dry ripening months. Mouse and weasel, ground squirrel and prairie dog, scampered their small, busy ways through the prairie's tawny nap. The prairie-dog towns stretched in unbroken networks underground for hundred of miles, shrill with the small, proud barks of the rodents. Only later, dispossessed by towns and farms, did they move to the high plains, where the grass grew in tough clumps from the harsher soil.

Long before the white men came plodding over the Alleghenies and poling along the rivers, the prairie was already well supplied with inhabitants.

Bighorns, North America's native sheep, grazed seasonally on the high western plains near the mountains. Pronghorn antelope, with powder-puff rumps alert to danger, ranged over two million square miles. The cougar, our American lion—call him puma, painter, catamount, mountain lion, as you will—stalked his kill where he chose.

Most important perhaps of all, the monarch of the prairie, the great American bison we call the buffalo, wandered across the land in vast, unnumbered herds. From water hole to water hole the herds often walked in single file. And the traces their hoofs hammered hard became

Above: Bighorn Sheep   Below: Pronghorn Antelope

Plains Indian Drawings—Hunting the Plains Animals

the trails later followed westward by the white men whose coming changed the world for all the prairie folk.

The prairie had known mankind for hundreds of years. But early men had fitted into Nature's plan without disturbing it. The Plains Indians, with their portable skin tepees, their feather headdresses, and their dogs, were still migrants like so many of the animals and birds.

Their villages did not disturb the prairie any more than did the prairie-dog towns. These Indians lived like the animals, taking what they needed to feed themselves, without greed, though sometimes, in years of plenty, with a free-handed lavishness. Their fires and their arrows combined brought down in their season even the monarch of the plains—the mighty buffalo.

It was on the buffalo that the lives of the Indians really depended. They feasted on fresh flesh after the hunt; the tongues and humps were considered special delicacies. They dried meat in strips over a slow fire to save for the long months ahead. But that was only the flesh. From the buffalo's bones they made ladles and needles; from his sinews, thread. From his wool, of a surprising softness, the women wove gowns and scarves and belts. From his hide

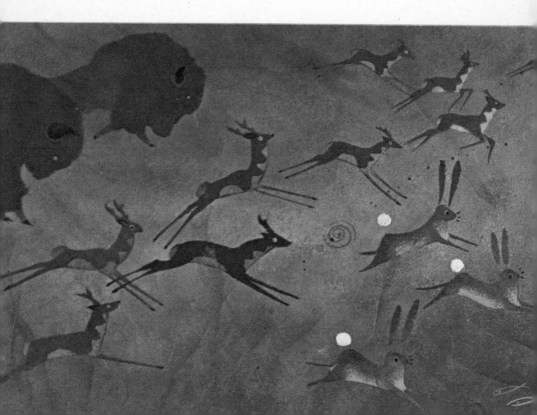

A Buffalo Family

came tepees, boats, robes, shields, and moccasins. Little wonder that prayers of thanks were offered to the spirit of the buffalo, that he appeared in art and songs and dances, that his horns were worn in certain ceremonials as a symbol of tremendous power.

Still the Indians, with all their hunting, did not cause any lessening of the numbers of the buffalo. A hundred years ago, when the white settlers started across the prairie, there were an estimated fifty to sixty million American bison alive. They had already been pushed out of the eastern forests by white men (the woodland buffalo had once ranged as far as Pennsylvania and Florida). Now, as the settlers came on in a thickening cloud, draining the marshes, ripping out the roots of the high, strong grass with the cutting blades of their plows, fencing the prairie and taming it, the days of the buffalo grew brief.

There was no peace anywhere for them. Now came the covered-wagon trains, the long lines of ox-drawn Conestogas, boat-shaped below, high-wheeled in back, with a soaring hoop of cloth on top shielding the seed of a home.

The buffalo looked up from their grazing as the wagon trains rumbled slowly past—patiently, until the crack of a rifle sent a fat cow toppling mysteriously to her knees.

Worse than the covered wagons were the lines of shining rails hammered down across the prairie floor. For it was the railroads that really doomed the buffalo. The men constructing the railroads hired hunters to supply their crews with meat, and the wasteful slaughter of the "cattle of the plains" began. Many buffalo were killed for choice steaks alone, some just for the much-coveted tongues, or

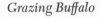

Grazing Buffalo

for hides. Countless thousands were shot solely for sport and left where they dropped for the glutted crows and coyotes and wolves to devour.

While the trails of the buffalo became wagon roads and the great grasslands Nature had given them for pasture were being plotted and surveyed, the buffalo, in a short fifty years, all but disappeared.

But it was not only the buffalo that felt the world falling away beneath their uneasy feet. The prairie dog, whose towns might stretch over the length of a hundred miles, now is seldom found in numbers except where land has been set aside as a preserve.

Prairie Dogs on a Preserve

The Cougar Keeps to Mountainous Country.

The bighorn also is now a fugitive. Once he wintered on the fringe of the rolling plains. But man's domestic livestock crowded him out of his original home, and natural enemies helped push him back to the last retreat of all—the rocky slopes of the mountains.

The cougar who hunted across the land has been driven into hiding too. The American lion, with a price on his head, moves like a silent shadow through the mountainous country bordering the plains.

Only on the high plains does the pronghorn antelope still range. A hundred years ago his species numbered forty million. Yet he came as near extinction as any—any except some of the birds.

Passenger Pigeons

Strangely, and sadly, it is among the birds that whole species have been lost to us. Though not of the prairie, the Carolina parakeet, the Labrador duck, the heath hen, all have been wiped out, their kind removed forever from the earth.

The lovely passenger pigeon, with its breast of rose, head of blue, and iridescent wings—this pigeon whose flocks numbering scores of millions darkened the sky as they flew, whose wings filled the ears with a tornado-like roar—every one is gone. It took a vast forest to keep them in food, for each bird of the millions ate a half pint of nuts and sturdy seeds every day. With the coming of man, of the plow, ax, and gun, the passenger pigeon vanished.

But there are birds on the prairie still. The wild swans

in passage float over placid prairie ponds, the grebes skitter comically along, and blackbirds swing in the reeds, nipping at ripened seeds. There are ducks of many sorts raising young among the grasses—mallard, teal, and pintail. There are owls and killdeer.

There are buffalo, too, a few still on the prairie—some five thousand of them in the United States, twelve thousand more in Canada. There are cougars and antelope and elk by the handful. A few of the children Nature placed here she has somehow spared from extinction.

It is their lives as they still live them today that we shall follow now. Here and there on the Great Plains of today, in out-of-the-way corners, the animals of old are still to be found, putting up their stubborn fight for survival. So our story is a living legend, its actors vanishing, perhaps, but far from vanquished still.

Trumpeter Swans on a Prairie Pond

Spring and the New Grass

THE prairie story begins each year anew with the spring thaw. For as the snow melts away to pools and slushy patches, the new grass appears. And to the prairie, grass is life.

Under the vast pale sky of winter's end, the huge tree-less reaches of the prairie quiver into life again. The hungry buffalo, nosing through the soft drifts to nibble bits of cured grass from last season, snuffle with pleasure at the unexpected sweetness of the first tender new greens. Antelope toss their delicate heads from side to side in an impatient search for the first fresh blades. The tough, low-growing buffalo grass, blue-spangled buffalo clover, even the silvery sage, which never changes color, have a young spring look.

From their underground burrows the prairie dogs, who have drowsed the winter away, scamper up to gather on sunny slopes, to see how the season is coming along. The sociable little fellows are eager for fresh grasses. They do such a thorough job of it, devouring roots, stems, and leaves of the grasses as happily as seeds, that the level ground around their burrows is often almost bare.

Prairie-Dog Baby

Buffalo in Spring

Soon a mild sweetness softens the air moving over the great plains. And swiftly, almost magically, spring has come—cloaked in a garment of grass. Across the low hills the soft green waves away to a horizon that seems to have no limit. Wild flowers—buffalo pea, gaillardia, portulaca, and bull thistle—dot the carpet with delicate strands of color. But to the prairie's grazing animals—the buffalo, the antelope, the elk, the prairie dog—it is the grass which is the rich assurance of food for the season ahead.

Prairie Wild Flowers

The Homecoming of the Birds

THE birds too have been watching the season's turn. In their various winter homes far to the south, they have been filled with an urge to travel. Through the winter many of the birds have led slow, quiet lives. But now, spurred by the lengthening daylight, the warmer weather, by a need for an abundant food supply, or perhaps by some inborn memory, new vitality surges through the small bodies.

This force is the beginning of the nesting urge, and it leads the birds across hundreds of miles to the somehow-remembered nesting grounds.

Though the game trails of old have been largely wiped out, still the invisible pathways of the sky, the flyways of the migrating birds, remain. They carry an almost endless traffic, going to and coming from warmer climes. Many birds return year after year to the very same meadow or plain or marsh. They may fly by day and rest by night, like the strong-winged loons and cranes and hawks, the swallows and swifts, which can feed as they fly.

Or they may fly chiefly by night, to avoid their enemies and to have time for rest and for feeding by day. So on prairie nights when the moon is bright, its beams may be blocked off by thousands of birds an hour streaking across the night sky. And down to the listener below will float the gabble of ducks or the haunting honk of geese. The homing flight of the wild geese is one of Nature's spectacles; their unerring sense of direction is one of her mysteries.

Ducks in Flight

A few birds may travel hundreds of miles without a stop, like impatient motorists. But most of them amble northward, averaging 80 to 120 miles a day, pausing for days of rest and feasting between flights. The time they take for their northward journey may be related to the speed with which spring moves up the land. Or it may be so regularly timed that it seems as if the birds kept calendars. They may fly foolishly into late blizzards and perish by thousands. But it still is a sign of spring worthy of rejoicing, as it was to the Indians long ago, when down to the reeds and grasses of the prairie marsh the returning waterfowl sweep.

For some the prairie marshes are just temporary stopping places on the long flyway leading at last to Saskatchewan or the treeless wastes toward the northern shore

Young Blue Heron in Nest

Migrating Trumpeter Swans

of Hudson's Bay. The sandhill and the whooping cranes, the great blue herons and the trumpeter swans, are bound for northern nesting spots.

But for many of the wild ducks, for the plover, the avocet, the phalarope, this is a joyous homecoming. Some of the impetuous ducks swoop down even before the last ice film has melted from the marsh.

Behind them the less impulsive geese glide cautiously down, wing feathers spilling the air gradually, broad feet spread to make the first contact with the waters of the marsh.

Now the serious business of the spring begins, the courting and pairing which is Nature's pleasant way of insuring the fulfillment of her purpose—the continuation of the species.

The courtship of the birds takes many colorful forms. One of the most fascinating rituals is the courtship dance of the whooping crane. Unfortunately this angular yet graceful fellow—standing almost as tall as a man, stalking majestically when he walks, flying with long neck straight outthrust and white wings spread seven feet across—threatens to disappear entirely. Despite his cautious habit of always having a sentinel on guard while the flock is feeding, his number had been reduced by 1953 to less than two dozen birds. A mated pair usually produces only

Rare Whooping Cranes

Sandhill Crane

one egg a year, and each spring the handful of survivors must make the long flight up from the Gulf Coast the length of the prairie to Saskatchewan; so the future of the whooping crane is precarious indeed.

His cousins, the smaller sandhill cranes, also perform an elaborate mating dance in the rose-streaked gray of the prairie dawn. According to an old crane custom, the male picks up a twig and tosses it up to express his admiration for a female. Once partners are chosen, the cranes bow to each other, then leap into the air with half-raised wings, hopping and bouncing across each other's paths in an ecstatic, if to us awkward, ballet.

Some of the birds have chosen mates in the south; others, like these cranes, do their courting along the way. They travel much of their journey in pairs. And when they reach their destinations they are ready to settle down. The ducks and geese, the coots and swans, may splash and squabble, but they waste little time before exploring the reeds for the best nesting places.

Meanwhile, on the broad reaches of the prairie itself, the dance of the prairie chicken is in progress. The American Indian, who knew his bird neighbors well, is said to have patterned some of his dances after the seasonal ritual of this bird and the other grouse. For the prairie chicken, whose short wings and heavy-breasted build make him ill-suited to long flight, is master of the dance and drum.

At sunrise, or even before, the prairie echoes to recurrent surges of booming sound. It is the prairie chickens, dancing on the jealously guarded bits of prairie each has chosen as his "booming grounds." With lifted wings, tail brush erect, and head lowered threateningly, each dancer

Sharp-Tailed Grouse

stamps his feet; and to punctuate his stamping rhythm, he booms. Between the upstanding black-and-white tufts on his neck swell gorgeous orange sacs that look like painted drums. As he expels air, the "drums" throb with a booming sound.

Two proud males face each other, while their drab females look on (for only among kingfishers and phalaropes do the females wear the brighter feathers and woo). They spring at each other in mock battle, whirling about in mid-air—and alternately, they boom!

Nearby the pompous sage grouse fans out his tail feathers and struts. He and his cousin, the sharp-tailed grouse, also dance about, pictures of self-importance, inflating the air sacs under their chins—a gorgeous purple in the sharp-tailed grouse—strutting and dancing to impress their quiet females.

Sage-Grouse Cock Strutting

But the season of courtship must pass for all creatures. Even the giddy aquaplaning western grebes, who delighted in skimming across the water in pairs, practically standing on their tail feathers—even they make homes and settle down. A grebe's nest is a floating island of reeds. Since all the comings and goings are by water, this bars most enemies. The grebe family hatches progressively, one egg at a time, so that mother often has the firstborn nestled on her back while she is still sitting on some of the remaining eggs.

Whenever the parent bird must leave the nest, she covers the eggs with cattails. This is partly for concealment, but also, more important, for warmth. Most mother ducks (whom grebes somewhat resemble) do not leave

Canada-Goose Goslings

Hungry Fledglings

the nest for long, nor do they go far. For a wing molting makes them flightless while their young need them. Thus Mother Nature assures her babies of care!

While the grebes prefer a protective moat around their homes, the tiny horned lark takes her chances on the open prairie, building her nest in a slight hollow in the ground, without even grass for cover. Her babies are fairly well concealed by their own earthy coloring while they lie there quiet. But the moment they hear Mother, trilling her long wavering twitter, *tee ti ti,* or guess that she is walking across the prairie toward them, they pop up like tiny Jack-in-the-boxes, a nestful of wide-open, hungry mouths. For almost more than any other kind of baby, bird fledglings seem to live to be fed.

In the spring
the prairie trembles
with new life.
Every shrub is misted
with small, fresh leaves,
every grass root
sends up fresh, sweet blades.
And among the grasses,
in the fragrant shade
of the prairie thickets,
quivering, alert,
the fragile prairie babies
face their new world—
dangerous but bright.

Prairie Babies

SPRING is the time for babies on the prairie. Mother Nature, it would seem, has taken into account the harsh demands of the prairie climate. To give each baby the fullest season in which to grow up to meet the harsh privation of winter, or to escape it by migration, mating seasons are so arranged that most of the babies are born in the spring. Thus the buffalo mate in July or August, elk in late September, bobcats, whose babies take only fifty days to develop, mate in January or February, prairie dogs not until April.

However long the babies have taken in coming, come spring the prairie is alive with them. Not many are to be seen at a casual glance, for the mothers do their best to keep their young ones safe from wandering predators hunting them—coyotes, badgers, eagles, and hawks.

When, in the spring, a mother antelope walks slowly, slowly toward a clump of sage, she is probably nudging before her an hour-old calf, wobbly and uncertain on its spindly legs, in its brand-new coat of spotted tawny brown. The mother will stand guard over her calf, nursing it frequently, barking to warn other mothers if danger approaches, for several days. As soon as the calf is strong

Doe and Fawn

enough to travel, the mother will patiently lead the way to the summer range, where she and her baby will join other mothers with calves, and some yearlings too.

The buffalo calf has a somewhat similar experience. No warm nest, no sheltered cradle, awaits the baby buffalo. In the days of old the long-grass prairie offered dim pockets of hidden grassy softness; but no more. When his mother feels that the time has come for his birth, she simply moves a bit away from the herd. The baby, in his shining wrapping or caul, drops to the bare ground. Swiftly the mother lurches to her feet and begins licking the membrane away from the baby's face, to give him a chance to breathe. Then she massages the small body with her tongue, to dry the damp new baby and to send the blood coursing through his young veins. By the time Mother has finished tidying up, so no hungry animal enemies would be drawn to the spot, the calf is ready to try standing up.

Lifting his weight on those brittle-looking legs is a real problem in balance the first few times. But hunger spurs the baby on, and soon he is nuzzling for his first breakfast.

Now we see that the buffalo calf looks a good deal like the domestic ones we know better. Its neck and legs are somewhat shorter. But it has scarcely a trace as yet of the heavy, humped shoulders of the grown buffalo. Its color is a bright yellow-red.

The calf does not have a long, pampered babyhood. Within two or three days it is strong enough to join the

Mother Buffalo Licking Calf   *(Below) Calf Trying to Stand*

Buffalo Calf with Parents

herd, which has been feeding close by. Close beside its mother, the calf keeps up as the herd rambles unhurriedly over its wide feeding ground. The mothers and their calves of several years back form the core of the herd. Young bulls often stay close to it too, with the older bulls ranging about the edges more independently and the oldest of the bulls leading solitary lives. These are the so-called "bachelor" buffalo.

With lots of calves, there are jolly games, stiff-legged running and butting games. And there is always Mother to run to for lunch and shelter, while the calf is small.

Within two months, a buffalo's babyhood is over. The

first bumps appear on the sides of the forehead, where the great horns will grow; shoulders begin to hump, and the reddish yellow of the baby coat deepens to brown.

But in spring the buffalo calves are babies still. And under the buffaloes' very feet the furry litters of the prairie-dog babies are drowsing along in their underground nests. Mother badgers are feeding their still-blind babies in underground, grass-nested burrows, too.

The cottontail rabbit mother has a nest prepared, but sometimes her babies arrive while Mother is not at the nest. Then she carries her pink, hairless new babies, as soon as she has licked them dry, one by one to the hollowed-out nest she has lined and blanketed with grass and downy fur. When the babies are safely covered over, Mother returns to her burrow nearby; from its safety she watches over her babies and tries to keep danger away.

Calf and Mother Buffalo

In sheltered dens or shady crevices in the rougher country, the cougar kittens are born. Two or three spotted, furry, one-pound kittens make up an average litter. After nine or ten days their eyes open and they are wide-awake, playful little fellows, scampering and scuffling roughly together outside their den.

It is often more than a full-time job for the mother cougar to keep them in food. For the first few weeks she must have meat for herself to keep up her milk supply. Then, when the kittens have been weaned, she must find them meat to eat and bones to chew.

Deer are her favorite prey. But they are watchful of ledges or trailside places where a cougar might lie in

Young Cougar Kitten

wait. And they are too swift for her to catch in a running chase. If deer cannot be had, rabbits, foxes, raccoons, or even porcupines will do. It is the way of Nature that some must perish that others may live. Often it is the weak or sick or old that are killed—Nature's way, perhaps, of keeping both hunter and hunted strong.

When the mother cougar makes a kill, she leads her kittens to it and joins them in the feast. If game is scant, they will return later to finish eating the kill. But if there is fresh food available, they much prefer it to leftovers. And there are always other hungry creatures glad to finish up what the cougars leave.

At about two months the cougar kittens will start going hunting with their mother. But even then they are far from grown up. Their mother will stay with them until they are almost a year old, to make certain that they are well fed and that they learn all there is for young cougars to know. By this time they will be half grown, large and slender, but somewhat clumsy, five to six feet long, including a lithe, long tail, and with soft fur dull brown or gray in color, paling to white underneath. But it is as chubby, spotted babies that they frolic in the spring.

Then too on the higher plains the slim, leggy, brown or tan pronghorn antelope fawns lie flat as dry grass patches on the open prairie. When their mothers come near, they totter to their feet to nurse; if an enemy approaches, they "freeze." Being, like deer young, with little odor, they usually are not found.

49

After a few days the fawns—they are often twins among the pronghorn antelope—join their mother's band and ramble up toward the high summer range. Before the years of the white men's great slaughter, antelope herds were as vast and numerous as those of the buffalo. Now the pronghorns are numbered by thousands instead of millions, but they, who alone of all our hoofed animals have lived on our continent for more than a million years, continue to go their way unchanged.

May and June are the nursery months on the prairie, and though cougar kittens thrive on tender fawns, though coyotes feast on ground squirrels and pocket gophers, though badgers delight in rooting out prairie dogs and eat birds' eggs whenever they can, though countless animals hunt the plump rabbit—still, if given a fair chance by man, every species manages to live on, in this hardy prairie world.

Pronghorn Antelope with Young

The Den on the Ledge

It is night on the prairie, the time for secret hunters. A slow, soft wind moves smoothly across the unbroken miles, swishing through the marsh reeds where the nesting birds sleep, hissing through the grasses where the long-eared hares play. Where the prairie roughens into upland, the night wind sweeps around rock outcroppings, sings through the needles of the pines.

It is there that the sleek mother cougar stalks. Smoothly, silently she moves with a gliding kind of gait. Yet within that grace almost two hundred pounds of power (the cougar is the largest of the cats in America north of Mexico) are tensed for attack. Hidden within those smooth-stepping paws are claws which can slash like needles of steel through flesh and hide. The mother cougar's small, sleek head holds weapons too—teeth like small ripping saws. Her skill at hunting made the Indian honor the cougar in days of old; but not so the whites, especially when it was their cattle she hunted. They placed bounties on her head, and drove her kind out of all the eastern states (but for a few spots in Florida) back into the rough western wilderness.

Tonight, at the start of her nightly hunt, she sharpens

Mother Cougar Stalks Her Prey.

Climbing Cougar

her claws on a nearby tree, then bounds lightly up its trunk. Belonging as she does to the cat family, the cougar comes by her tree-climbing talents naturally. She does not plan, as many people think, to wait on an overhanging limb to leap down onto her prey. Too many of the deer and other animals are on guard against this trick. Instead, she uses the extra elevation as a vantage point from which she can scan the countryside, looking for deer or other moving creatures—even a stray young buffalo.

Tonight's hunt may not bring her such prey; she does not average more than a deer a week. But now she is not hunting for herself alone. Behind her in the shadows trail three hungry kittens out on their first real hunt. She must find them something, if only a rabbit or raccoon.

She cannot hope for help in feeding or in training from the kittens' father. It is only among coyotes and wolves (and birds) of the prairie folk that the parents stay together to raise the young. She and the father of these kittens were together for only a couple of weeks. If he came back now, she would not welcome him. He might even try to attack the kittens. She will feed them and train them herself.

Behind her, the kittens break into a noisy scuffle. They will never surprise any game this way! The kittens, their baby spots just fading from their furry coats, are by no means born hunters. Their claws are sharp, their eyes are bright, but all the ways of quiet patience, the tricks

Cougar Kittens

of timing, the fine skills needed for keeping alive—all these they must learn, and rather slowly too!

Now their mother with a signal quiets the children down. She has heard a small movement in the night. Nearby through the darkness a deeper shadow flashes. It is the jackrabbit. Now he pauses to browse in a juicy herb patch. Soundlessly, without warning, the cougar is upon him. He has not a second for fear or pain.

At last there is meat for the kittens, though really not enough. They growl and tear eagerly at their meal until scarcely a scrap remains.

Now they cuff at each other again in rough play. They scramble out on tree branches—and even at this age their claws support them well on the steepest climb. For a moment Mother joins them in their play, for she likes a good romp too. But one over-ambitious small fellow tumbles from a low cliff. Before he has stopped rolling in the dust below, his mother is at his side, licking him, nosing him tenderly to make certain that he is safe.

Soon the pangs of hunger once again cut the playtime short. There was not enough food to satisfy the kittens. Mother cougar had scarcely a bite herself. Now she moves away again into the night.

Almost directly in her path, a fawn freezes in the grass. Instinctively it knows it must stay motionless. One false move—just the flick of an ear—and it is doomed. However, a fawn is practically without scent. The cougar at night depends largely on scent, so the fawn still has a chance.

The Cougar Leaps on Her Quarry.

The cougar, almost as if some sixth sense tells her that the prize is near, circles the spot where the small fawn waits—circles and returns. But the fawn waits, motionless as a stump. The cougar moves on again. Death leaves this little corner of prairie grass.

The cougar safely out of range, the tiny fawn springs into life and runs to its mother for reassurance.

The deer treads lightly when a cougar is near—if the deer knows. But sometimes there is no warning. The cougar's quick grace, her ability to move swiftly and silently, is fatal. The final dash on the drowsing, unwary deer is made in twenty-foot leaps—with all the suddenness of the thunderbolt.

The cougar, after a first few ravenous bites, drags the carcass to a secluded place. Then she rounds up her kittens and leads them to the scene, and at last the family eats its fill.

When they have gorged on all they can hold, the mother thriftily covers the rest of the carcass with twigs and grass, saving it for a later time, when she and the kittens will return for another meal. If food were always to be had for the hunting, she would prefer a fresh, warm kill every night. Coyotes and bears might have her leavings then. But this season things are not that easy. Her

Cougar Kittens Share in the Kill.

kittens must learn to make do with what they have.

The young cougars, light-hearted and playful, little dream how many lessons they have to learn: that to see a deer, even a fawn, is not to catch it. That even the best-aimed leap may miss its mark. That a cougar is no match for the heel-flashing speed of a deer in full flight.

No animal lives a more paw-to-mouth existence than the young cougar during his first season on his own. These youngsters will find that out when they are a year old and their mother sends them off to be independent because she will soon have new babies to feed. Sometimes the juniors learn to travel and hunt together. But even co-operation does not always produce much by way of results. Hunger forces them to include some odd items in their diet—frog legs, for example, if they are quick enough to catch the frog. During their first hunting sea-son, they are inclined to chase anything that moves. If starvation threatens, even porcupines are fair game. A cougar may learn to flip the porcupine over on his back with a swift swipe of the paw, in order to get at his defenseless under side. But the porcupine has his own defenses. He can stiffen his back and present his barbed quills to the intruder—or he can climb a tree. Getting him cornered is no easy task.

Sometimes a tree squirrel looks like easier game. Still, it takes an agile cougar to catch the average red squirrel. Out along the branch the cougar creeps. But at his first slip, the squirrel scampers off to the safety of a far-out

Half-Grown Cougars

twig, where it sits and chatters an alarm. The young cougar may as well relax; he drops to the ground and sheepishly ambles away.

In salmon country there is one more chance for the young hunter. The headwaters of a salmon stream in spawning season are a cougar's banquet spot. For these salmon, home from the sea, have finished their life's work. They have exhausted their energies in swimming up the river; they have laid and fertilized the eggs to insure another generation. Now, their mission accomplished, their life cycle complete, exhausted beyond recovery, they await the end. For some the end comes in the form of a hungry cougar, a cat turned fisherman.

Many indeed and strange are the ways in which Nature provides for her children in seasons of hardship!

Before the stern advance
of Man, with his sharp-
toothed harrow and his
deep-bladed plow,
the prairie dog
has retreated,
across the prairie
and down the years.
His towns, which once
dotted the prairie,
sometimes covering
a hundred miles apiece,
have shrunk to the
scant dimensions
of Man-granted preserves.
But the merry little fellows
continue to go
their cheerful, sociable ways.

Prairie-Dog Town

OVER the prairie in the soft morning sunlight hovers a light blanket of sound—a pleasantly sharp small chirring that ripples and falls. On the almost level surface of the prairie itself there is not much to suggest a town with thousands of inhabitants. The grass over a wide area is nibbled down to the roots, and scattered about are the small shadows of tunnel doorways, each doorway circled with a dike of earth as much as two feet high. These dikes have been tamped into shape with care by the small inhabitants we now catch sight of, sunning themselves companionably and conversing in small chirps.

For this is a prairie-dog colony, and by these dikes, or their absence, you may judge the experience of the homesteader below. If it is a young householder's first burrow, the dug-out earth may be loosely scattered; a wiser builder, saddened by experience with prairie floods, will have a firm, stout, circular dike.

But the open doorways with their dikes give no impression of the city itself. It lies several feet underground. In the old days it is said that a single prairie-dog community might stretch more than a hundred miles. Even now, when prairie dogs have been all but exterminated by man, with his bullets, poison, and traps, the maze of tunnels and chambers may occupy a vast stretch of prairie.

The prairie dog's burrow is one of the most complex in nature, an intricate system of intersecting tunnels, dead-ends, and escape exits. There are also bedrooms with cozy grass nests in which the babies spend their first weeks of life—usually at least seven weeks.

Mother of course goes up every day for her meals. By early summer the babies are ready for a first excursion into the unknown world above. Mother has chosen a fine sunny day—high wind or rain would keep the whole village indoors. She has been up for an early look around and found the town already abustle with neighbors out

Prairie-Dog Babies in Their Nest

to enjoy the warm sunshine. So she leads the way up the sloping passage; at the guardroom, a few feet from the doorway, she pauses to listen carefully. No cry from above warns of danger nearby. No snuffling or digging suggests an attack. So on she goes, up to the sunshine.

The babies scramble after her, sometimes climbing over each other in their eager haste. Mother has been

Prairie-Dog Babies Out-of-Doors

weaning them, cutting their nursings short, so they are all hungry, and where Mother goes they will follow as fast as they can, since to them she means food. But that is not Mother's plan for them today. Having them hungry is the best way to get them to try the sweet young grass waiting overhead.

Out they tumble onto the open prairie, aquiver at the

newness, the strange smells and the brightness, after their world of dark. They chase here and there, bursting with excitement, knocking each other over, having a wonderful time. Some see Mother nibbling at grass stalks and follow her example. One little fellow who does not like the idea of a change in diet snuggles up to Mother for his familiar lunch of milk, but Mother pushes him gently away. He must learn to like the new grown-up diet along with all the others.

Watchful Prairie Dog

Prairie Dogs Are Sociable.

While the family munches, Mother keeps a wary eye out for danger. For the prairie dog's enemies are too many to mention: coyotes, hawks, bobcats, swift-digging badgers, and sleek black-footed ferrets who can slither down the prairie dog's hole as neatly as a rattlesnake. The babies must learn to watch for these dangers; until they learn, Mother watches for them. She never nibbles for more than seconds without rearing up on her small, plump haunches for a sharp look around. If anyone, even another prairie dog, seems to threaten, she gives her yipping alarm call. This sharp little call says, "Danger approaches!" and the prairie dog almost flies to pieces with the excitement of saying it. He also "barks," and it is this habit of barking which has given the prairie "dog" its name. Actually the little creatures are rodents, cousins to the gopher and the tree and ground squirrels.

Everything is exciting to the merry prairie dogs. They will never outgrow their sociability, and all over town there are chirping conversations going on as the grown-ups visit and lunch, enjoying the sun or taking time out for a soothing dust bath.

To the young, everyone is an exciting stranger. Imagine finding folks who are not prairie dogs!

A mother cottontail and her furry young ones sit quietly for a moment while the prairie-dog babies run about them and stare; then the bunnies go on with their face-washing lessons—a mystery and delight to the little prairie dogs.

The young burrowing owls mystify them too. And indeed it does seem strange to think of bird families which insist upon living underground. Actually the owls do not do their own burrowing. They like to find an abandoned prairie-dog house to take over for their own. In under-ground nests their young are hatched and spend their first few weeks.

Now that they have moved up, like the prairie-dog young, to take their meals on their earthen doorstep, some instinct tells them that even the ground is not their proper home. They spend long hours stretching their wings, hop-ping and frantically trying to fly.

When the young prairie dogs come to call, the burrow-ing owls hold themselves aloof. They do not welcome visi-tors to their home—not even the family that lived there

Prairie Dog Meets Baby Burrowing Owl.

before. There is an old legend that burrowing owls, prairie dogs, and rattlesnakes live in harmony in the same burrow. The harmony, the friendly sharing, simply are not true. Burrowing owls will not move in unless the prairie dogs have moved out; and if a rattlesnake slithers down, probably looking for a spot for a nap, the "dogs" will leave fast enough—and stay away until the snake has gone.

Now Mother Owl shoos the visiting prairie dogs back toward their own burrow. The prairie-dog mother does not interfere. This is all part of their training in How to Be Prairie Dogs. They must learn, for one thing, to stay near home for safety's sake. And they must learn to get along with their neighbors, each on his own terms.

If the pocket gopher is digging a new burrow, and does not want the neighborhood kids in the way, they will find it out soon enough. They may find the whole procedure of excavating new and fascinating, but the gopher, with a bit of rough and tumble, soon shows them that he is serious and sends the young prairie dogs on their way.

Even among other prairie dogs, the young adventurers get into trouble now and then. For there are strict boundaries in prairie-dog town. If a stranger strays into another family's territory, or wanders too close to the wrong doorway, the owner sets up a shrill barking, almost throwing himself up into the air as he cries, just as their own mother might: "Stay away! This spot is mine!"

To the bewilderment of the youngsters who meant no harm to anyone, the many voices become a chorus. At every burrow doorway, it seems, the owner flings out his or her small chest in a dauntless territorial cry.

The youngsters learn their lesson, one of the first laws of a well-regulated prairie-dog town. It is a good thing to know.

They must also learn the urgency of the shrill alarm call. Many a prairie dog, old and young, has lost his life by not heeding this warning and running for his burrow swiftly enough. The animal who does reach his burrow takes up the alarm call, too. Soon all are yipping. At last, with a final flick of the tail, and a final bark, each householder dives into his burrow and safety.

This time it is a badger, one of the prairie dog's worst enemies since long before man came along, who threatens the town. Low-slung, powerful, determined, the badger

Badger, a Sober Hunter

can outdo even a prairie dog in digging speed. Chances are the prairie dog can outrun the badger on the surface, if it has a good start. But this stocky, grumpy, clumsy-looking fellow, twice the prairie dog's size (badgers are more than two feet long) and many times its weight, is fairly speedy, and an all-too powerful digger to suit the prairie dog.

Young badgers may gambol about, and even seem to dance in season; but grown-ups are likely to be sober about their business of hunting, anxious to store up a good layer of fat before the winter comes. When a serious-minded badger comes along, the prairie dog is lucky who has escape tunnels waiting, lightly plugged with earth, so he can speed out the back door and safely sit beside it, watching the badger burrowing in the front.

Some badgers have been known actually to dig prairie dogs out of their holes; they are not to be taken casually.

71

Black-Footed Ferret

Even worse, from the little fellow's point of view, is the black-footed ferret, arch enemy of all prairie dogs. This relative of the weasels is rarely seen these days. Slim and elegant in appearance, with his sleek fur coat of light brown, his black fur boots and goggles, the black-footed ferret used to be an unwanted dweller in many a prairie-dog town. When prairie dogs began to thin out, the black-footed ferret, dependent upon them, almost vanished.

The prairie dog, whose only defense is to hide, has little protection from a hungry hunter like this, one who can follow him right into his home. When a ferret comes in, all the prairie dog can do is stir up the family and try to speed away. Now his elaborate system of tunnels proves its worth. For every tunnel is equally full of the aroma of tender prairie dogs. The hungry ferret cannot tell which way to go. He may even find himself back at one of the exits before he catches up with a single bite of dinner.

When a rattlesnake happens along, the prairie dogs are no better pleased, but they are less frightened. They know the ways of the rattlesnake. They know that a snake can strike half his own length away. So with amazing courage they dart about, staying just out of range of those dangerous fangs. The adult prairie dogs are almost too big to make an appealing meal for a rattler. But he would dearly like a couple of the youngsters.

"Chirr-yip!"

All over the prairie the cry springs up. Mother Prairie Dog herds her babies down the tunnel at the sound of the general alarm. One baby is missing, wandering after a distant blossom. Mother gives one sharp call, races after him, and shoos him toward the safety of home. But

Young Prairie Dog

before she can get back herself, the danger is upon her.

It is a coyote, clever and persistent hunter—today a very hungry one, too. He has cut Mother Prairie Dog off from her burrow. Now, nose to the ground, he chases her as she runs frantically, searching for any burrow entrance, across the rough ground.

Cornered at last, Mother Prairie Dog stops, whirling to face her foe. As long as she can face the coyote, she has a chance. For the last thing the coyote wants is those razor-sharp teeth sunk in his nose! He has met prairie dogs in battle before and he does not relish the idea of making a direct attack.

Alas, prairie dog! Breathless and frightened, she seems hopelessly outmatched. Yet she will not give up. She even makes an occasional small charge of her own, setting the coyote back on his heels. Then, as the coyote, almost play-

Prairie Dog Holding Off Coyote

fully biding his time, circles her slowly, drawing closer and closer, she bares her shining teeth, darts her bright gaze about—and makes a break for freedom, past the coyote's shoulder.

It's a desperate try. But it succeeds. In a flash she is over the dike and down her own burrow, down deep enough so the angry coyote's digging cannot even rattle dust down on her babies and her.

The coyote, outwitted and no less hungry for the chase he's been on, is in a mood to chew up anything he finds in his path. What he finds is the slow-moving rattlesnake that so recently caused a flurry of fear.

Again the coyote, with delicate footwork, circles for the best position. Instinctively he takes advantage of a weakness of the rattler: the snake cannot see movement directly above his head. The snake strikes—but the coyote's

Coyote Outwitted

quick reflexes take him out of reach. Now it is his turn to attack. Darting in above the snake, taking advantage of his blind spot, the coyote tries for a hold directly behind the snake's head. He circles a few times, then, clamping his jaws, the coyote snaps back his head and flings the snake onto the rocks. Down he pounces once more—and the battle is over.

As the reptile's coils relax in death, the coyote wanders off. Close behind him all over the prairie, small furry heads appear, bright eyes darting their glances this way and that to make certain the prairie is clear. They cannot be too careful, for prairie dogs' enemies come from all sides—from underground, along the surface, and even from the warm, bright air above.

Down from the sky at lightning speed plummets the deadly prairie falcon. Cold of eye, with a hooked bill designed to rip soft flesh, the falcon is a swift and relentless hunter, related to the hawk. He can strike almost before his presence is known. But, aware of the alarm system of the prairie-dog town, he often comes in low, almost at grass-top level, sneaking up for his first strike, a blow designed to stun his prey.

Then in mid-air he brakes to a stop, circles swiftly, and drops upon his dazed victim, sharp talons ready for the pick-up. During this moment, it may be, the "victim" will gather his wits and tumble into his burrow. For a prairie dog must know all sorts of tricks to live long in prairie-dog town!

Time of Drought

Summer settles heavily down upon the prairie. Hot, dry
winds lick up the moisture from the soil, crumbling it to
pale dust. As the earth parches, the grass dries and withers,
the green carpet of the prairie yellows and wilts. The
water holes of the antelope and buffalo shrink and dry up.
Over the whole prairie shimmering heat waves dance
under the blaze of the sun.

Now the prairie dogs' midday naps grow longer; they come up early in the cool of the morning, and again toward sundown. But the baking sun of the midday hours they try their best to avoid.

Jackrabbits spend the long bright days quietly in the shady shelter of their "forms" in abandoned burrows, hollow logs, or thick tangles of underbrush. Even though they may have nests of babies nearby all through the sum-

Cottontail Rabbit

Prairie-Dog's Home . . .

mertime, barely hidden in their shallow beds, the mother never nurses them during the day. She scarcely stirs out by daylight except perhaps for a dust bath now and again.

The prairie dogs enjoy dust baths too. And so, to the sorrow of the prairie dogs, do the lordly buffalo. The trouble with the buffalo's dust bath, from the prairie dog's point of view, is that the buffalo all too often takes it right on top of the prairie dog's burrow.

As the prairie scorches, flies and mosquitoes and sharp-pronged seeds bite into the buffalo's shaggy hide, almost bare where the long winter hair has dropped off. The buffalo is in great distress. The cowbirds are of consider-able help; they feed on the bothersome insects on his hide. But even the cowbirds cannot soothe the tremendous itching now.

As the big creature wanders along, switching his useless little tail, what should he spy, in his dim-eyed way, but a mound of earth which he can pulverize for a dust bath.

The buffalo lets down his two thousand pounds or more, clumsily, onto his front knees. Then over he rolls, squirming and kicking until both sides of his coat have soothing dust well rubbed into them.

By the time a few more buffalo have followed him, the once-neat dooryard of the prairie dog will be flattened out like a great, rough-edged saucer ten feet or more across—a true buffalo wallow filled with churned-up dust.

... Becomes a Buffalo Wallow.

Poor prairie dog! At this season even without the buffalo he is always busy repairing his walls. For the dry earth crumbles easily enough without the clomping of huge hoofs or the steamroller treatment of a squirming buffalo.

Week follows dry and parching week. Sometimes the air presses heavy, dry, and still against the crumbling ground. Again a hot breeze stirs and twists, sending "dust devils" spinning many feet into the air, but bringing no cool relief.

Every water hole in the vicinity has dried to a muddy pool, trampled about by the countless feet or hooves of thirst-troubled animals. The buffalo can stand thirst better than domestic cattle, but now they must have water. So they begin their dusty trek.

Old trails cut generations ago by the huge buffalo herds still lead them, down steep bluff banks, across rough, broken countryside. Sometimes they travel single file, patiently following their leader in a slow, plodding march across the parched countryside. Day after day the herd pushes on, heads drooping, short tails thrashing futilely to try to keep off the flies.

At last, across the distance, to their nostrils comes the smell of fresh water. Up come the heavy heads; the nostrils quiver. Is it a spring, a stream? It does not matter. It is water, the life-giver, instinct tells them. Like a churning brown tide they plunge forward at a gallop. Recklessly they plunge ahead, holding their footing on steep trails, leaping from high banks, till they come at last to the river.

River it is—a broad brown stream soon muddied by the tramplings of the herd. There is water aplenty here for all, and enough to share with the natives too, with the deer and antelope and elk.

So the weary buffalo come at last to the end of their wanderings.

Buffalo Herd at the Water

Fury and Fire!

WE might think the buffalo could find peace with fresh grazing beside a well-filled water hole. But as the summer heat wears on, a strange restlessness, a gnawing hunger, overcomes the herd. The bulls become ill-tempered; they stand apart, glaring at their fellows. They paw the earth and bellow their challenge to the world at large.

As tempers shorten, here and there a young bull tries

to push his way into a group. Perhaps a pawing snort from the great, bearded master may be enough to discourage him. If not, there is trouble ahead. For the mating battles are on.

The bull, moving restlessly among the cows, filled with a vague general anger, fastens his small, hot eyes on the rival. Down goes his head. The pointed ends of his short, curved horns tilt menacingly toward the enemy.

With a bellow of rage the great bull is upon his young rival. Cautiously the younger bull retreats. Not driven completely from the herd, but put in his place at least, he lurks about the outer fringes, watching the brewing storm.

Now two great bulls square off in a sham battle. Or is it sham? Will one give way before the threat of those black horn-points facing him, backed by more than two thousand hard-driving pounds? They bellow and snort

Battle of Bulls

and paw the earth into a hot dust cloud. The cows nudge their calves away a safe distance.

This is a contest of mighty wills; but neither bull gives in. As if at a secret signal, both lunge forward. With a crash the two great, hairy foreheads meet—bone on bone. Now, in a flood of rage, they back away, bellowing, then lunge again.

The great horns hook viciously, trying for the opponent's eyes. Crash! Snort! And away they back once more, remarkably light-footed for beasts weighing more than a ton. The objective of the battle is to outflank the enemy, catch him if possible off balance, and then to smash into

A Buffalo Duel

Prairie Lightning

his side as he lies on the ground and to gore him.

This duel ends at last in the retreat of one warrior as he staggers off, defeated. But the fever has spread. A huge dust cloud rolls up as nearly every bull in the herd is drawn into the fray.

As the battle subsides, sometimes after weeks of intermittent duels, the losers retreat, their eyes glazed with shock. The winners, scarcely less battered, round up their cows and settle down to placid calm once more.

The calm is soon shattered, though, by a blast from nature itself. Under the scorching sun of summer, the heated plain has become a vast tinderbox. The dry, crisping grasses seem of themselves about to quiver into smoke. A single bolt of lightning can set them aflame. And now across the vast sky tumble black clouds—the huge and terrible beauty of the thunderheads sets the prairie aquiver.

As the clouds roll on, a black-velvet menace, between them lightning crackles and flashes. Then the after-crash of thunder seems to split the heavens.

The buffalo paw the ground in terror, as the distant thunder prods them on. Now crackle! crash! above their heads the air masses collide in a shattering roar. Panic seizes the buffalo. Even their stately leader lowers his head and rushes blindly forward. The herd follows, pushing, shoving, running, rushing—a rocking sea of humps.

Behind them the worst, it seems, has happened. A lightning bolt has struck the prairie. In seconds, flames are licking over the landscape. Ugly yellow-gray smoke climbs the sky. The dry, hot wind whips the flames through the grass, surrounding nests and trapping countless small prairie folk. In the face of the onrushing, licking flames, the only hope is in flight.

Birds Escape the Prairie Fire.

Dry Wind Whips the Flames.

Down go the prairie dogs, underground. Up go the larks, the cowbirds, the blackbirds and grouse and magpies. In flocks they seem to explode from the grass, winging out ahead of the flame. Here a breathless badger lunges along, just keeping pace with the fire. There a confused rabbit bolts back into the wall of flame—and escapes, singed but otherwise unharmed, across the charred ground beyond. Antelope too take to their heels in panic.

And all this is too much for the buffalo. Their flight from the terror of the thunder now turns to full stampede.

Even the youngest calves must keep up with the pace

of terror or be crushed beneath pounding hooves. If they can, they place themselves ahead of the running adults and race along, almost setting the pace of the herd—if not being pushed. On sweeps the herd, mile after mile, in a blind madness of power and speed. They have long since outdistanced the menace of the fire; but nothing can stop them now, neither river nor ravine.

Far behind the buffalo, the fire races on. Night comes, and the flames glow murkily against a smoke-stained sky. Dawn finds animal survivors clinging to shelters in the rare prairie ponds, resting on the far shore of the great river which the fire could not leap. Still the flames eat on, without pause or pity, sometimes for several days. Eventually, their fury spent, the crackling of the flames dies to a sputter in which only sparks and embers flicker and dance. And these in their turn die too.

Silence comes to the blackened prairie, rest and the first sense of healing power, as the prairie moon begins its great circle across the huge dark sky.

High Water

THE prairie fire has burned itself out at last, and the hot breezes of the following days have whirled off the last lurking threads of smoke.

Back to their old homesteads drift the survivors. The prairie dogs have come up for a discouraging sniff around. Not a blade of grass seems to be left them, and unlike many of their relatives they have no pantries stocked with

91

seeds on which to fall back now. Dinner-time looks a long way off to the hungry prairie dogs.

Other prairie folk too are drifting back. A jackrabbit (really a long-eared hare) sprints across the charred plain, his long leaps covering fifteen to twenty feet. Now and again he seems to take an extra spurt in midair. This extra surge has a special purpose; it is his "spying hop" whose added height and distance give him a chance to check on any pursuit. Now he is looking for a tangle of unburned sagebrush in which he can fashion himself a new shelter.

The cottontails come back. Some start courting at once with their "bunny hops," in which one rabbit leaps up in the air and the other runs underneath. And next month the mothers will have new nestfuls of babies to watch over and to feed.

The coyotes prowl the burned-out prairie, sensing that these others will be back, without nests in which to hide.

Coyote Hunting

Prairie Rainstorm

And still the sun, the baking sun, beats down, while under the hard, dry surface, the grass roots are stretching down, down toward moisture almost too deep to reach.

At last the wind changes. Huge puffy thunderheads roll once more across the prairie, blocking off the sun. Dark shadows race over the ground; a yellow-green light fills the waiting day. The first thunder-clap mutters after a lightning flare. The clouds seem to lower, then dissolve in a pulsing torrent of rain.

The parched, stone-hard ground cannot soak up this treasure as fast as cloudfuls fall. The precious rain stands in pools on the surface, trickles down shallow slopes, runs along the gullies, gathering into bubbling, rushing rivulets

Bedraggled Porcupine

as it seeks out the coulees and the valleys. Soon it is a raging, many-armed flood.

The prairie rivers fill and overflow. The marshes stand reed-top high in water. Nests which have been sheltered in the cattails go swirling off. Baby birds, flooded out of their homes, cheep in damp despair.

All the ground dwellers are in danger now: the cottontail with her babies nested down in the old burrows, the badgers, the porcupine, the jackrabbit. Everyone is seeking some high, safe perch—the rattlesnake and coyote too. There are not enough high spots to go around. Everyone who can swim (and most of the prairie folk can, in a real emergency) is swimming now; and if you spy a floating log, you do not give too much thought to who else may be using it with you. Some unaccustomed neighbors, like a badger and a soaked porcupine, may rest from their struggles side by side.

Each high point of ground soon becomes an island, with murky waters swirling all around. Exhausted by swimming and fighting flood currents, even a jackrabbit and a rattlesnake may rest together peacefully here.

Their rest is no longer very peaceful after some coyote pups arrive. These are a bedraggled-looking group, these usually carefree youngsters who only yesterday were happily playing near their den, letting Mother work overtime to furnish their meals. Now they are hungry again, and cold and wet. Mother should be doing something about this, they feel, so they set up a howl for her.

Rabbit and Rattlesnake Escaping Flood

Hungry Coyote Pups

The long, damp fingers of the flood reach the prairie-dog colony, too. Now those who worked hard at their dikes receive their well-earned rewards. The waters are stopped behind those walls. On their still, safe, little mounds the prairie dogs wait, watching the waters rise.

The lazy or inexperienced ones who did not take time or put enough work into a good, firm tamping job pay the price now. For the water soon trickles through inadequate dikes. Once the flood seeps down the sloping tunnels into the nests below, all is lost. There is nothing to be saved but the family itself—and everyone scrambles at top speed to the surface then.

Flooded out, marooned on their tiny islands, the unlucky ones wander in a daze, not knowing which way to turn. There is only one course, it seems, left to them—to strike out for higher land. So, much as they dislike the water, they swim for their little lives now.

Like most of Nature's creatures, the prairie dogs can swim, if their lives depend on it, even though not accustomed to water. Soon a bedraggled little group haul themselves up onto higher ground and begin to shake and comb themselves dry.

But to a prairie dog, the worst state of all is to be without a home! The little fellow's only refuge, remember, is to go underground. So as soon as the ground is firm enough, instinct tells the refugees what to do: dig themselves new homes.

There is no time for uncertainty; everyone begins to dig. Their busy back feet push up the moist earth, as tunnels deepen and rooms round out. Then the tossed-up earth must be tamped into place by brisk little noses, to form the base of new dikes. Almost frantically they dig; energetically they tamp, keeping one eye out for danger all the time.

Dirty faces they do not seem to mind, but they do mind having sharp digging paws clogged with mud; so now and again they take a moment off to clean their paws. Then back they go to digging and pounding, until the moon rises on the neatly diked doorways of a snug new prairie-dog town.

Stealing down from
the wooded high country,
with its steaming lakes
and snow-hung trees,
down from the rocky ridges
and the blanketed hills
comes winter—
whistling shrill warnings
across the prairie world.
Behind its white veil of beauty
the prairie creatures see
the skull face of winter,
time of hunger, time of pain.
They turn their backs
to the icy blasts,
patient sadness in their eyes.

Time of Frost

By the time the first chill autumn rains have soaked the prairie from low, gray, windy skies, a touch of frost has reached the high country. There the cottonwoods shiver with leaves of gold; and in the chill morning air there is a silvering of frost shimmering on the grass.

Autumn seems to have touched the bighorns too, in their steep summer pasture range—touched them with

100

madness, perhaps from the harvest moon. For eleven months or more of the year, the bighorn ram is a very sheepish sort of sheep. He ambles around in a leisurely way, chomping on grass, climbing now and then to some inaccessible-looking ledge, but in general avoiding the use of too much energy.

Autumn, though, brings the mating season, and with it a kind of frenzy overcomes the bighorn rams. Other beasts may do battle for their mates, winner taking all. Not so the bighorns. They simply seem to enjoy knocking their heads together, and that is what they do, day in, day out, in the most skull-cracking style.

Two rams square off; with lowered heads they lunge together. Crash! go their skulls, and shock waves ripple visibly down their spines. Back up. Take aim. Crash again! The hollow crack of horn against horn echoes from every cliff.

Yet it is a pointless battle. It begins over nothing, it settles nothing. The ewes, in whose honor the battle is presumably staged, pay little attention; in fact their placid expressions suggest that they find the whole thing rather silly.

But the males, knocking heads in an endless game, seem to have forgotten how to stop.

Fortunately, Nature takes care of that. At the first sign of a floating snowflake, they must think of leaving this rugged land for milder winter pasture on the fringe of the Great Plains.

Down from the crags the bighorns come; from the foot-hills the elk and the deer drift to lower altitudes. The last leaves shiver and fall to the ground. On the pines, the needles shake under the wind's chill blast.

The first snow drives the prairie dogs underground temporarily, though since they do not really hibernate they often come up briefly on sunny days. In their nests in the tangled underbrush the rabbits and hares fluff out their fur and settle deeper into the warmth.

Rabbit at Burrow Doorway

Winter Comes Down from the Mountains.

Overhead, the cold days and nights echo to the haunting cry of the geese, beating their way southward in great windswept V's. Waterbirds leave the freezing ponds where food supplies now are scant. Meadow larks and other blackbirds—almost all the feathered folk—whirl away in noisy southbound flocks.

Now the wind howls in wild new earnestness, flattening cattails and frosty grasses, slashing a knife-edged blast of snow across the prairie's face. The gray sky lowers. The fine flakes fly. Drifts whirl and tower under the wind. Soon all the familiar landmarks disappear beneath the blanketing white.

Elk Herd in a Blizzard

Down from the Arctic sweep winter's bitter winds; from the vast plains of Canada they bring the icy blizzard. Before the slash of the wind and the sting of snowy needles, the grazing herds upon the prairie gather closer together and bow their heads, facing the time of hunger.

Not a blade of grass remains in sight. There is little enough of the tough prairie scrub. Winter is a bitter season, pale with hunger for the antelope, the buffalo.

The coyote, too, wanders lean-ribbed across the empty drifts. Some may die before the spring brings back their food supply.

Still, through the blizzard drifting deep, the buffalo herd plods its lonely way—a symbol of the courage, the quiet fortitude, which, given the sympathy of Man, will keep all these creatures of Nature's prairie from vanishing quite away.

Buffalo Herd on a Winter Trail

Glossary

antelope — *see* pronghorn antelope.

antler — one of the horns, or a branch of one of the horns, that grow from the skulls of all male and some female deer. Solid, bony organs, antlers are shed and grown again each year, and are used for butting other stags.

avocet — a wading bird from 15 to 18 inches long, related to the snipe. It has black and white plumage, bluish legs, webbed front toes, and short tail and wings. To get its food, primarily shellfish and insects, it sweeps its long, curved bill through the water. The avocet usually nests on swampy ground.

badger — a member of the weasel family, about 28 inches long and weighing about 15 pounds. Thick-set, it has short legs, and, on its powerful front feet, long claws for digging. Its coarse fur is gray with black and white markings across the head. Badgers try to avoid trouble, but can be stubborn fighters.

bear — a large mammal with a heavy, massive build; a short tail; thick, shaggy fur; five powerfully clawed toes on each foot; and a solid tread. Omnivorous, bears eat chiefly fruit, roots, insects, honey, fish, and other animals. They hibernate in winter. Commonest bear of North America is the black bear. The grizzly, weighing up to 1,000 pounds, now remains only in the Rockies.

bighorn — also known as Rocky Mountain sheep. Its length is about 5 feet, its shoulder height about 40 inches, and its weight about 350 pounds. Bighorns

have grayish-brown hair with a white patch above the tail and black horns and hoofs. Males have large horns that curve backward; the females' are much smaller. These horns are never shed. Bighorns eat grass and twigs. They are very agile.

blackbird — a common name for several largely black, related birds, including the cowbird, the red-winged blackbird, and the meadow lark. The males of one species, Brewer's blackbird, have entirely black plumage.

black-footed ferret — a now extremely rare member of the weasel family. The adult males, somewhat larger than the females, are 20 inches or more in length. The ferret is yellowish brown above and creamy yellow below; it has a black band across its eyes, black feet, and a black-tipped tail. A predator of small animals and birds, it is especially fond of prairie dogs and is sometimes called "prairie-dog hunter." The ferrets usually live in abandoned prairie-dog holes.

107

bobcat — also known as bay lynx and wildcat. About 36 inches long and about 20 pounds in weight, it has grizzly, rufous-brown fur and a very short tail. Bobcats eat birds and small animals, preferably cottontail rabbits. They do most of their hunting at night.

buffalo (plains) — a once-abundant subspecies of the cud-chewing cattle family. American buffalo are really bison rather than buffalo because they have humps over their shoulders, which the true buffalo of Asia and Africa do not. The males are very large, sometimes weighing more than a ton. The females are smaller. Both sexes have horns that are never shed, but the males' are much larger.

Their shaggy, dark-brown coats are shed during the summer. Now under government protection in the western U. S., buffalo live in herds and eat mainly grass.

buffalo (woodland) — a bison larger than the plains bison and with a darker-brown coat. This color difference is probably due to diet, since the woodland buffalo eats herbs, mosses, and pea vines, as well as grass.

buffalo grass — a low-growing perennial grass found in the western U. S. where the buffalo used to graze.

buffalo pea — a trailing and climbing American vetch with bluish-purple flowers.

buffalo wallow — the depression made on the prairie by the rolling of buffalo in the dust.

bull — the adult male of buffalo and certain other animals.

bull thistle — a large wild thistle with purple heads and prickly leaves.

bunch grass — any of several grasses of the western U. S. Bunch grass grows in clumps that form thick turf.

burrow — an underground home, usually with passages, made by digging animals.

burrowing owl — also known as ground owl. About 9 inches long with a small head and long legs, it has brown back feathers with tan spots and white underparts with brown spots. These owls use abandoned burrows for their nests and eat small animals, birds, and insects. They can see in the daytime as well as after dark.

calf — the young of certain animals, such as buffalo and antelope.

Carolina parakeet — a now-extinct bird, having been widely killed by man. It was 13 inches long with green feathers on its body and a yellow head. It had a cream-colored, curved beak. It was not a prairie bird.

cattail — a common, tall marsh perennial with long, flat, narrow leaves and a brown flower spike.

coot — a bird also known as mud hen and water hen. About 16 inches long, it has slate-gray feathers that are darker on its back. Coots spend most of their time swimming, although they can also run and walk. They are usually found in shallow ponds or marshes, frequently with ducks. Their nests are built in reeds.

109

cottontail rabbit — sometimes known as gray rabbit. The adults are about 18 inches long. The color of the some 27 species and subspecies in the U. S. varies according to the environment. They usually have grayish-brown fur on their backs, white fur underneath, and short, puffy, white tails. They eat in the morning and evening and spend the rest of the day in their burrows. The females have two or three litters of four to six babies a year. The newly born are helpless, shut-eyed, and hairless.

cottonwood — any of several species of poplar growing along the water courses of the western U. S.

cougar—also known as panther, puma, mountain lion, painter, and catamount. It is a member of the cat family. Adult males may be 7 feet long and weigh as much as 200 pounds. The fur is tawny brown above and dirty white below. The long tail is tipped with black. Cougars hunt mainly at night, killing cows, sheep, colts, small animals, and particularly deer. Man is their only enemy.

covered wagon — also known as Conestoga wagon and prairie schooner. A broad-wheeled wagon covered with canvas, it was especially suited for traveling across soft soil and was used by the pioneers migrating westward. The original covered wagons were made at Conestoga, Pa.

cow — the adult female of buffalo and certain other animals.

cowbird — the smallest blackbird (about 8 inches long). Males are greenish black with distinctive brown heads and breasts; females are brownish gray. A parasite, the cowbird usually lays its eggs in the nest of a smaller bird. The young cowbirds generally monopolize the nest and the attentions of the foster mother to the detriment of the latter's own offspring. Cowbirds follow buffalo and domestic cattle to feed on the insects these larger animals attract.

coyote – also known as prairie wolf. Members of the dog family, coyotes are about 4 feet long, weigh between 30 and 40 pounds, and have gray or tawny fur. Although mice are their staple food, they eat a wide variety of small animals, including calves and lambs. They usually hunt in pairs, but when after antelope or deer they may travel in packs. While hunting they howl frequently. They are skilled in avoiding traps.

crane – a large wading bird of the marshes and plains, having a notably loud cry. When in flight cranes extend their necks to full length. U. S. species include the sandhill crane and the whooping crane.

deer – a member of a family of cud-chewing hoofed animals. The adult males of most species (and the females, too, in a few cases) have antlers that are shed each fall and renewed each spring. During the summer the antlers growing in are very tender and are covered with hair. By fall they are full grown and the deer has rubbed off the "velvet." The antlers are used in mating battles. Deer eat mainly grasses, twigs, and foliage. The mule deer and the white-tailed deer are two common American species.

den – the hole or burrow of a wild animal.

dike – a bank, especially of earth, thrown up to form a protective barrier.

duck – a member of a large group of migratory waterfowl found in all parts of the world. Most have strong wings, short legs placed far apart and well back on their bodies (hence the "waddle"), and webbed front toes. Skilled swimmers and divers, ducks are usually divided into three main groups: river, or fresh-water, ducks; sea ducks; and mergansers. The river ducks include the teal, pintail, and mallard.

dust devils – small spiraling columns of dust.

eagle – a large predatory bird belonging to the same family as hawks and kites. Dark-brown, powerful birds with keen vision, hooked beaks, and sharp talons, eagles soar with their long wings held horizontal. They build their nests at the tops of tall trees and on inaccessible cliffs. The bald eagle, our national emblem, has a white head and white tail.

111

elk — also known as wapiti, one of the largest members of the deer family. The adult males are about 8 feet long, weigh from 600 to 800 pounds, and have large, deciduous antlers. Elk have coarse, long hair of yellowish or brownish gray, and shaggy manes. Summering in the mountains and wintering in the valleys, they eat leaves, twigs and grasses. They are very graceful.

ewe — the female sheep.

fawn — a young deer in its first year.

fledgling — a young bird that has just acquired his first flight feathers.

flyway — the entire range that birds of a particular kind inhabit. It includes their nesting places and their winter homes, as well as the migration routes connecting these two areas. There are four great flyways in this country: the Atlantic, the Mississippi, the Central, and the Pacific.

form — the bed or the hidden resting place of a hare or other animal. It is frequently in the underbrush or a hollow log.

fox — a member of the dog family. There are three principal kinds in North America: the red, kit, and gray. The adults are about 3 feet long to the tips of their long, bushy tails. Consumers of small animals and fruit, they are famous for their swiftness and cunning.

gaillardia — a plant also known as blanket flower. It has bright yellow and red long-stemmed flowers.

goose — a bird related to the ducks and swans. Geese have longer legs and walk more readily than ducks, and have shorter necks than swans. There is no difference in coloring between the males and females. Some common native species are the blue, the snow, and the white-fronted, and the Canada or common wild goose.

grass — any of a family of plants with narrow, spear-like leaves and hollow, jointed stems. They are eaten by grazing animals, and also by man—for example, cereals, sugar cane.

great blue heron — sometimes known incorrectly as blue crane. The largest American heron, it attains a length of up to 50 inches. Great blue herons have grayish-blue feathers, with some black on their wing tips and back, and crests of plumes on their heads. Their long, pointed yellow bills snap fish and small animals with lightning speed. Solitary birds except during their mating season, they build their nests usually in trees, frequently in colonies.

grebe — a skilled water bird. It tries to escape from its enemies by diving and swimming underwater. Though short-winged, grebes are excellent fliers. They have very small tails and use their lobate feet as a rudder when they fly.

ground squirrel — a burrowing member of the squirrel family. More than 30 species occur in North America, some resembling the tree squirrel, some the chipmunk. They eat seeds, roots, grasses, insects, and mice. Some hibernate.

grouse — a rather large, fowl-like, terrestrial game bird protectively plumaged in brown, red, and gray. Most species have completely feathered legs. Grouse eat seeds, berries, insects, and snails. Generally polygamous, the males perform unique courtship rituals, including dancing, strutting, booming, and drumming. Among the U.S. species are the sage grouse, sharp-tailed grouse, and prairie chicken.

hawk — any of numerous birds of prey which hunt during the daytime. The hawk has sharp claws with which it kills small animals and reptiles. It then tears its kill to pieces with its sharp, hooked bill. Hawks are usually large birds, from 11 to 24 inches long. Some of the common ones are the red-tailed hawk, the goshawk, and the marsh hawk.

heath hen — a now-extinct grouse. The adults were about 17 inches long with rusty-brown feathers on their backs and rusty-white feathers underneath. They nested on the ground. They were the eastern form of the prairie chicken.

herd — a large assemblage of animals.

hibernation — the habit of certain animals, such as bears, some rodents, and rattlesnakes, of spending the winter in a more or less dormant state.

horn — a growth from the head of an animal, used chiefly as a weapon. Mammal horns include: the permanent, unbranched, hollow sheaths growing over a bony core, found on bovines; the branched, bony, deciduous antlers of deer; and those of the pronghorn, which have characteristics of both types.

horned lark — also known as the prairie horned lark, being a year-round resident of the prairie. About 7 inches long, horned larks have brownish-pink backs and white feathers underneath. On their chest and around their eyes they have black patches. On their heads they have black feathers that often stand up, resembling little horns. They nest on the ground and eat mainly seeds.

jackrabbit — also known as long-eared hare. Large hares with long ears and strong hind legs, the long-eared hares weigh from 6 to 10 pounds and have keen senses of sight and smell. When running from danger they can leap from 10 to 15 feet high. Their homes, merely a shady spot in the underbrush, or in a hollow log, are called forms. Here the young are born, already well developed and with open eyes. U. S. species include the black-tailed and the white-tailed.

killdeer — also known as kill-dee. The killdeer is a plover that gets its name from its cry. About 10 inches long, it has a greenish-brown back, white underparts, and two black bands across the head and two across the chest. Its main food is insects.

kingfisher — usually, in the U.S., the belted kingfisher, a 12-inch-long blue-gray bird with a large, crested head, a long bill, and rather short wings. A fish-eater, it dives, often from a height of 50 feet, into the water to catch its prey.

kitten — the young of the cat family.

Labrador duck — a now-extinct sea duck, once common along the northern Atlantic coast but exterminated by man for its feathers. About 29 inches long, the males were black and white; the females, grayish.

litter — a group of baby animals born at one time of the same parents.

long-eared hare — *see* jackrabbit.

loon — a member of a genus of large aquatic birds. Loons are generally blackish or grayish above and white below; during the summer their dark feathers are touched with white. Web-footed, they are skilled swimmers and divers, using their long beaks to spear fish. Loons have an eerie cry. They usually live alone.

magpie—a large (20-inch-long), glossy-black and white bird with a very long tail. Related to the crows and jays, the two magpie species are common residents of the western U. S.

mallard — a common, large fresh-water duck, 22-24 inches long. The males have green heads with white rings around their necks. Their backs are brownish gray; their chests, purplish; their underparts, gray. They have blue wing patches striped with white. The females are mottled brown. Mallards are very hardy and are a favorite game duck. They eat small animals, wild rice, insects, and plants.

meadow lark — a common migratory North American blackbird, about 10 inches long, with a black-and-brown-streaked back; a black crescent on its yellow throat; and white outer tail feathers. The western species has a particularly musical song.

migration — the movement of large numbers of animals from one place to another, such as the seasonal migration of birds from summer homes to winter homes. In North America this movement is generally between north and south, and between high and low altitudes.

molting — the shedding and renewing of such parts as the outer skin, feathers, hair and horns of an animal.

mouse — a small rodent. Of many species, mice adapt well to a wide variety of environments. They have soft fur, long, scaly tails, and short legs. By nature shy and peace-loving, they are eaten by almost all carnivores. Their only defense is alertness to the many dangers that surround them. They are very prolific.

owl — a chiefly nocturnal predatory bird common almost throughout the world. Owls have large eyes that are directed forward, a disk-like arrangement of facial feathers, a hooked beak, and soft plumage that renders flight noiseless. They comprise two families: (1) barn owls and (2) all other owls.

passenger pigeon — a now-extinct bird, exterminated chiefly by man. Passenger pigeons were about 17 inches long and had bluish-gray feathers on their heads and backs, and reddish breasts.

phalarope — a member of a family of shore birds. From 7 to 9 inches long, the adults have thick plumage, long bills, and long legs. The females are larger than the males and have more colorful plumage. After the courtship, in which the female is the aggressor, the male builds the nest and hatches the eggs.

pintail — a large fresh-water duck with a small head; a long, slender neck; and, particularly in the male, a long, pointed tail. A swift flier, it seems to leap into the air when taking off. The male has a brown head, gray back, and rufous, green, and black patches on the wings, which are edged with white. The female is mostly brown.

Plains Indians — also called the Buffalo Indians. They are the tribes that lived on the Great Plains of the U. S. and Canada, depending on the buffalo for their food, shelter, and clothing. They were largely nomadic, although some tribes engaged in agriculture to a limited extent.

plover — a small shore bird famous for the long-distance migrations of some species. Plovers have small, plump bodies and

116

long, pointed wings. The golden plover, probably the best known of the family, breeds along the arctic coasts of North America, then migrates across the Atlantic to Brazil and Argentina. In the spring it returns to its breeding grounds in the Arctic by way of the Mississippi Valley.

pocket gopher — a rodent also known as prairie pocket gopher and red pocket gopher. It is chestnut-brown and about 11 inches long. Its front feet have large claws for digging. It has large fur-lined pouches, opening on the outside of its cheeks, in which it collects food. Pocket gophers spend most of their lives in underground tunnels, from which they feed on the roots of plants. They are eaten by hawks, owls, foxes, bobcats, snakes, and other predators.

porcupine — a rodent about 3 feet long and weighing about 30 pounds. It has long grizzly

fur scattered among many barbed spines. These spines, which can be raised by muscular contraction, are loosely attached and can easily be stuck into an attacking animal. Consequently, porcupines have little to fear from most animals.

portulaca — also called rose moss. A small annual plant, it has brilliantly colored blossoms, either single or double, that usually open only in the sunlight.

prairie chicken — a member of the grouse family, about 18 inches long and weighing about 2 pounds. Its back is yellowish brown spotted with black; the underneath feathers are white barred with brown. The tail is short and rounded, and there are feather tufts on its neck. The bird eats insects, fruit, seeds, and grain. During the mating season it "booms" and drums.

117

talons. Its back is brown, and its breast is white spotted with brown. The male is 18 inches long; the female, 20. Prairie falcons eat birds and small rodents, especially ground squirrels.

predator — one that plunders or destroys, particularly an animal that kills and eats other animals.

prairie dog — a member of the squirrel family. About 14 inches long, it has reddish-brown fur on its back and yellowish-white fur underneath. In the winter it is pale buff. Its tail is short. Prairie dogs dig burrows for their homes and live in large colonies.

prairie falcon — a bird of prey. A member of the falcon family, it has a powerful build, long wings, hooked beak, and strong

pronghorn antelope — often called the American antelope.

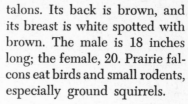

The pronghorn is not a member of the true antelope family of Asia and Africa, but is a strictly North American animal, intermediate between deer and cattle. Its horns consist of a horny sheath over a core of bone, like those of antelope, but they are shed annually, like those of deer. The female's

118

horns are either smaller than the male's or absent. Pronghorns have tan backs and, on their rumps, a patch of white hair that stands up when they are frightened, warning other antelope of danger. They have two white bands across their throats and chests and have thick manes. Their horns and hoofs are black. They eat grasses and other plants.

raccoon — a medium-sized nocturnal carnivore. It has a broad head, short legs, and long yellowish-gray hair with a black mask across the face and black

rings about the tail. It builds its nest in a hollow tree. Raccoons eat small animals, grains, fruits, and nuts. They like to wash their food before they eat it.

ram — a male sheep.

rattlesnake — a thick-bodied poisonous snake of North America. It has rattles at the end of its tail. Each time it sheds its skin, a new rattle grows. The prairie rattler is yellowish green with dark spots on its back.

red squirrel — a medium-sized tree squirrel, generally rufous-colored above and with a broad, bushy tail. About 20 species and subspecies are found in North America. Living chiefly on nuts, they are active all year round.

reed — a tall grass that grows in wet places. There are several kinds, some of which have jointed bamboo-like stems.

rodent—a member of the group of gnawing animals, the largest order of mammals. Rodents have bright eyes, sharp ears, and vegetarian tendencies. They include rats, mice, squirrels, beavers, porcupines, and, in some classifications, hares and rabbits.

119

sagebrush — low shrubs abundant in the western U. S. Their silvery-gray leaves have a sage-like odor and are sometimes eaten by browsing cattle. The wood from these shrubs burns readily.

sage grouse — also known as sage hen. It is the largest member of the grouse family. The males are from 25 to 30 inches

long; the females, about 20 inches. The back of the sage grouse is black, brown, and yellowish white; the belly is black; and the wings are shorter than the tail. The bird is feathered down to the toes. During the mating season the males strut. Sage grouse eat the leaves of the sagebrush.

salmon — a large, marine game fish that mates and lays its eggs in fresh water. The young eventually work their way down the streams to the sea. When ready to breed they return to fresh water. The Pacific salmon generally die after breeding. The salmon's flesh is usually orange or pink when cooked.

sandhill crane — a large wading bird, about 4 feet long and with a very large wingspread. Its feathers are bluish gray; its bill and feet, black. Sandhill cranes eat insects, small animals, grain, and roots. Like all cranes they stretch out their long necks in flight and utter loud cries.

sharp-tailed grouse — called also the pintail grouse. A grouse resembling the prairie chicken but distinguished by its pointed tail and absence of neck tufts. About 20 inches long, these

birds have yellowish-brown feathers touched with black on their backs, brown and white feathers on their chests, and white feathers underneath. They also have feathers on their legs. They dance during their mating season.

species — a biological classification lower than a genus and higher than a subspecies or variety. It includes plants or animals that have in common certain characters distinguishing them from all other, similar groups.

squirrel — a member of a widely distributed family of small rodents that includes the arboreal squirrels (the red and gray squirrels and flying squirrels), ground squirrels, chipmunks, and prairie dogs. All members have rounded, bushy tails.

swallow — a bird famous for its graceful flight. From 5 to 8 inches long, swallows have large mouths, short bills, long wings, and forked or notched tails. Their legs are short, and their feet are used for clinging rather than perching. They catch and eat insects while they are flying.

swan — a large water bird, generally pure white. Swans are related to the ducks and geese.

They have very long necks, which may be even longer than their bodies. They eat seeds and water plants. Native species include the whistling swan and trumpeter swan.

swift — generally a smaller bird than the swallow, measuring from 5 to 7 inches long. Swifts love to play while they are flying. They never perch but cling, usually to vertical surfaces.

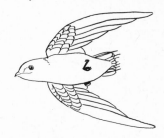

Their tails are short and are used for support when the birds are clinging. Swifts eat insects, which they catch in flight. They use a secretion from their salivary glands as cement in their nest building.

teal — the smallest of the ducks and a very fast flier. Teals include the blue-winged and green-winged teals, the latter occurring the farther north.

tepee — a conical tent, usually made of buffalo hides, used by the Plains Indians for homes.

121

territorial call—warning call or cry given by an animal when another animal, usually of the same kind, enters the area surrounding his home.

thunderhead—the large, white and dark cumulus clouds that appear before a thunderstorm.

tree squirrel — any arboreal squirrel.

trumpeter swan — a large, fresh-water swan. White, with black beak and black feet, it may be as long as 5˙feet. Because trumpeter swans are so easily seen, most of them have been killed by man.

weasel — a member of a large genus of small carnivores. Long, extraordinarily slim, and short-legged, weasels in summer are generally brown above and white below. In winter most of those living in regions of snow turn completely white, except for a black-tipped tail, and are then called ermine. Skillful, savage hunters, weasels tend to kill every small animal within their

reach. The weasel family includes badgers, minks, otters, skunks, and black-footed ferrets.

western grebe — a large water bird, member of the grebe family. Its feathers—dark above, satiny white below—have been so valued for coats and capes that the bird has been exterminated in some areas. The chicks ride on their parents' backs under the wing coverts.

whooping crane—a large, white bird with dark-green bill and black legs. Some are almost as tall as men. Today these cranes are becoming extinct because man has killed so many, and because the female usually lays only one egg a year.

wolf — a large mammal belonging to the dog family and resembling the German shepherd dog. Carnivorous, it eats rodents, deer, and so many domestic animals that it is much hunted by man. Believed to be monogamous, wolves live in dens in family units while the pups are small. Common American wolves include the gray, or timber, wolf and the coyote.

yearling—a young animal in its second year of life.

Index